An Essential Guide for the ESFJ Personality Type

Insight into ESFJ Personality Traits and Guidance for Your Career and Relationships (MBTI ESFJ)

by Samantha Treimon

Table of Contents

Introduction

The ESFJ personality type is often referred to as "The Caregiver." People belonging to this group are known to be warmhearted, loving, and service-oriented. Being sensitive and naturally altruistic, these individuals have a knack for perceiving what other people need, even when they don't say it out loud. ESFJs thrive in harmonious environments and will work to make sure that a peaceful and pleasant atmosphere is encouraged and preserved.

Did you know that learning about your personality type can help you make better life choices, including those about your career and even romance? If you've recently used the Myers Briggs Type Indicator (MBTI) psychological assessment tool and found out your personality type is ESFJ, then be prepared to learn a lot more about yourself here. The information within this book will not only help you to get to know yourself better, but it will also help you choose the right career path, and make better choices when selecting a romantic partner.

Described as Extroverted, Sensing, Feeling, and Judging, the ESFJ personality type is truly one of the best personality types. Extroverted means you are friendly and sociable. Sensing means you are grounded and practical. Feeling means you are empathetic and perceptive. And Judging means that you are organized and disciplined. Nevertheless, these words do not sum up the ESFJ personality type. There is so much more that you need to know in order to maximize your potential as an ESFJ, so let's get started!

Chapter 1: Understanding the ESFJ Personality Type

The ESFJs are those individuals that everybody seems to like. If they can, they will try to make everyone around them happy. These unique individuals are natural cheerleaders, inspiring people to do better and to always look at the positive side of things. They are the 'life of the party' and they literally bring sunshine to every room they wander into.

Friends and family of the ESFJ will always benefit from their supportive attitude. These individuals are always ready to lend a helping hand. They just need everyone around them to be happy and they can sense if ever something is amiss. The ESFJs are not ones to just stand around when they see or feel that something is wrong, though. These folks will actively work to remedy the situation or if possible, solve the problem.

Many ESFJs have a flourishing social life. This is due to their warm-heartedness, genuineness as people, and their innate ability to reach out to those they meet. They are popular and well-liked in their communities. Individuals that belong to the ESFJ group are not shy people. They enjoy the spotlight and they see this as a chance to bring happiness to those around them. For instance, the ESFJs enjoy organizing social gatherings for their family, friends, and workmates. Whether it's a small tea party, a big business meeting, or Thanksgiving dinner, the ESFJs find pleasure in planning and participating in the get-together. Emceeing for gatherings, volunteering for games, and getting the ball rolling are tasks that almost always fall to the ESFJs. And the best thing about that is that the ESFJ person will do all these with aplomb! While many will let old friendships fade, the ESFJs take time and effort to stay up-to-date with their friends' lives. They do this not only because they don't want to lose their friends, but mainly because they have real concern for what's happening in the lives of the people they care about.

The ESFJs are known for being practical. As a result, they won't find scientific theories and age-old philosophies interesting conversation topics. For the ESFJs, real life situations such as those seen in the news or those happening in their community are far worthier topics to spend time on. Their interest in real life events stems from their desire to help out and be able to contribute something. The ESFJ folks are traditional and they prefer to live by the set laws. They are not experimental nor are they open-minded about doing things their own way or according to their personal beliefs.

For most ESFJs, their sensitivity can be the greater challenge that they need to overcome. And while their ability to perceive the feelings of others makes them good friends and family members, the ESFJ can sometimes become too concerned about what others think about them. As a result, they have a tendency to feel insecure about themselves, and this puts a strain on their overall self-esteem. People in a relationship with an ESFJ should always be ready to provide positive affirmation in order to counter this effect. For the ESFJ, he can prevent these blows to his self-confidence by accepting the fact that he has no power over other people's thoughts and feelings.

Chapter 2: The Strengths and Weaknesses of an ESFJ

Sometimes, the fastest way to learn about a person's personality type is by enumerating his strengths and weaknesses. However, the fastest way doesn't necessarily mean the best way. The best way is still to spend time with the ESFJ in your life and learn about all the things that make him a special person. Nevertheless, here is a guide on the strengths and weaknesses of the ESFJ personality type.

The ESFJ Strengths

Good Leaders

For certain, the ESFJs make good leaders. They have no problem connecting with people and inspiring them to think positively and achieve more. But what really makes the ESFJs effective leaders is their strong practical skills. They thrive on routines and they are very efficient when it comes to completing day-to-day activities.

Responsible and Reliable

The ESFJs have a strong sense of duty. They never take their responsibilities lightly. People can always rely on them to complete their tasks and to do their share of work. But in the case of the ESFJ personality type, not only do they take care of their load; they also go out of their way to help others complete their tasks either by doing extra work or by inspiring them to work harder.

Loyal and Trustworthy

People with the ESFJ personality type give very high importance to stability and security. Because of this trait, they can remain loyal to people they believe in. In addition, they would rather maintain the current state of events, especially if the circumstances are pleasant and satisfactory, rather than cause or support trouble that could result in instability and uncertainty.

Warmhearted and Perceptive

These two traits go hand in hand in making the ESFJ a great helper to those around him. He is very perceptive to the needs of others as well as to their emotions. And his kindheartedness allows him to act on his perceptions.

Easily Connects with Others

Individuals that belong to this personality type are naturally friendly. They don't shy away from opportunities to meet new people and they certainly make sure that they connect with whoever they interact with. As a result, those that make an acquaintance of the ESFJs feel instantaneously at ease with them—like they've already known them for a long time.

The ESFJ Weaknesses

Needs to Be Liked

For all the good that the ESFJs do, they are still worried that some people may not like them. Social status seems to be a crucial element to the happiness of the ESFJ. At times, their decisions in life can be affected by their concern for what others will think of them. If the ESFJ does not overcome this weakness, he may be putting a limit on his own development and progress. Also, his self-esteem may never be stable for as long as he worries about the opinions of others about him.

Strict and Too Traditional

One thing that the ESFJ isn't is unconventional. These individuals are firm believers and followers of rules and traditions. They are set on the orthodox ways of doing things and they might have some trouble accepting changes. While this may not really be a problem in general, there are times when the ESFJ will try to impose his beliefs on others. Some people may find this unreasonable and even annoying. Perhaps the reason why the ESFJs do not readily accept new ways is due to the fear of appearing unknowledgeable or unskilled about something. As a result, they stick to their comfort zones.

Sensitive to Criticism

The ESFJs are very sensitive. They have a tendency to get offended easily whenever they hear criticism from their family, friends, colleagues, and superiors. They have some trouble handling criticisms no matter how constructive they may be.

May Get Clingy or May Try Too Hard

People with the ESFJ personality type thrive on praises and recognition for their good deeds. Once they feel unappreciated, they may try harder to get the praise they need. Some people will regard them as being clingy and can label them as people who try too hard to win applause.

Too Helpful

When the ESFJ sees someone in need, he readily offers helps, even when they didn't ask for it. Some people will appreciate this trait but there are those that just want to be left alone and may not appreciate the help given by the ESFJ. Some will even regard the ESFJs as someone who is being helpful to the point of becoming too intrusive.

Although these are the typical traits of the ESFJ personality type, every individual has a unique background and have undergone different experiences, therefore, if you have an ESFJ in your life, you can use this guide to understand his personality. However, nothing beats getting to know the real person. Get to know the ESFJ in your life and discover his unique traits.

Chapter 3: The ESFJ as a Friend or Romantic Partner

It's not difficult to know what kind of brother, friend, or lover the ESFJs would be. They are unselfish people that are always willing to make the people they care about happy. As friends or lovers, they will always go out of their way to show their support and love. As family members, they are caring sons, daughters, and parents. People in a relationship with an ESFJ will never feel bored around them because they will do practically anything to see a smile on the faces of their lover, family, and friends. Relationships have a great importance in the lives of the ESFJs. They deeply care for others and they also need to feel loved and appreciated.

The ESFJs as Friends

Individuals that have the ESFJ personality type are the kind of friend that works to stay in touch with the people they care about. They will call weekly just to catch up and they will always remember birthdays and special days. They make time for their friends and they make sure that the friendships they have do not just fade away. ESFJ friends are trustworthy and loyal. They will stand by the people they have faith in and they can always be relied on to provide emotional as well as other kinds of support.

For the ESFJ, friendship is very important. People that have this kind of personality type are traditional and they expect to keep the traditions of friendship. For these individuals, helping out a friend is both a pleasure and a duty. Because they are kindhearted and devoted, they will always be there for their friends. However, they will also expect the same kind of dedication to the friendship from their friends.

Meeting an ESFJ for the first time is usually a pleasant experience. They have the ability to make anyone feel at ease right away. And when they become close friends, the ESFJs make an effort to make everyone around them feel comfortable and happy. ESFJ friends don't like arguing, especially when it's about differences in principles. They will avoid joining in conversations about topics that they do not agree with and might even try to change the topic or the atmosphere of the room if they sense that it could lead to arguments and conflict.

ESFJs make wonderful friends because they inspire those in their circle to do better, achieve more, and always look at the bright side. Due to their ability to perceive their friends' feelings and unspoken desire, the ESFJs can sometimes manipulate others into taking steps towards directions they did not originally think about. Fortunately for the friends of the ESFJs, these individuals are sincere, kind, good people so they will always try to lead their friends towards betterment.

The ESFJ as Lovers

Folks with this personality type make the best partners. They are loyal, warm, and caring to their lovers. They are also a traditional bunch and so they will give utmost importance to respecting the commitment made between two people that love each other. They will observe the traditional ways of keeping a romantic relationship and they will shower their lover with devotion.

People that are in a romantic bond with ESFJs feel secure because these individuals can be very dedicated in the relationship. They are sensitive to the needs of their partner, they are caring, and due to their power to perceive, they are able to provide whatever their lover requires to be happy. Because they are traditional and a little old-fashioned, the ESFJs don't take romance lightly. For them, love is not something to be played with. They will treasure the whole experience and they won't regard another person's ngs carelessly. For the ESFJ lover, romantic relationships are never casual. In romantic relationships, their goal is to settle down, start a family, and be with the right person for the rest of their lives.

An individual that just wants to play around and take things easy may not be a very good match for the ESFJ. Persons with this personality type will take dating as well as every stage of the courtship very seriously. They want someone who is on the same page with them when it comes to the book of love.

The ESFJ lover wants mutual love, respect, and support from his partner. But aside from these, what the ESFJ really needs from his mate is reassurance that he is loved and appreciated for the things he contributes to the relationship. Although arguments and conflicts are part of all relationships, the ESFJ may not be able to handle these situations very well. Any lover of the ESFJ will need to be careful when criticizing their partner. ESFJs are very sensitive and they can easily feel hurt when they hear disapproval and reproach from people they care about.

Loyalty is one of the positive traits of the ESFJs and it greatly benefits their relationships with others. In romantic relationships, the ESFJs honor their commitments and they work hard to keep their partners happy. In return, the ESFJ lovers need to feel the same kind of devotion from their partners. It's also important for the ESFJs to feel that their husband, wife, or lover supports their goals and ambitions. For the ESFJ, that's a crucial factor in a successful relationship.

Chapter 4: Choosing the Best Career for an ESFJ

With a clear idea about the strengths and weaknesses of the ESFJs, it's now easier to determine what career paths the ESFJ should take. And while every person has the freedom to pursue a career that he likes, taking this useful information into consideration can help you find happiness and fulfillment in your professional life.

What Careers Are Best for ESFJ?

Due to the ESFJs desire to make everyone around them happy, it's easy to see them taking up leadership roles. But that's not the only reason why. The ESFJs are diligent and they have the capability to get things done. They are also charismatic, often inspiring people around them to strive and achieve more. They are sociable and they have people skills, so they can easily get along with a large group of people. The ESFJ individuals are also perceptive and sensitive so they can provide the needs of their subordinates.

The ESFJs will do well in jobs that require structure. These individuals are very organized and they like to keep things in order. ESFJs also find pleasure in working on tasks that have clear and predictable steps. They like security and stability so they find routine work not at all unpleasant.

Careers in accounting can be a good match for the ESFJs due to their reliability and practical skills. However, keeping the ESFJs behind the desk or buried in paperwork may not be a very good idea as these individuals are extroverted. They need to still be able to have interactions with their colleagues. Therefore, careers in Human Resources are also good options for the ESFJs. Other jobs where the ESFJ can fit in are customer support, where they can talk to people and help them with their complaints. They will also thrive in sales as they have a natural talent for winning people over with their charm and sensitivity.

Individuals with the ESFJ personality type are good listeners. This trait coupled with their sensing power make them good counselors. They can provide beneficial advice to those in trouble because they are warm, kind, perceptive people. ESFJs thrive in jobs that allow them to meet new people, talk to them, and create meaningful relationships. If they have a job that allows them to socialize freely, then they can be happy with that kind of work.

Although they can make good leaders, the ESFJs can also choose a work in non-managerial jobs. This is because they have great respect for structure, tradition, and authority. ESFJ workers want to feel stability and security in their jobs. Naturally, they support authority and they are comfortable with it. The ESFJs may not really enjoy jobs that require analytical thinking. They prefer to work on tasks that require practical skills and allow them to get out of the office and interact with other workers.

Here are some professions that match the ESFJ personality type:

- Counselors

- Therapists

- Social Work

- Teacher/Trainer

- Nursing

- Doctor

- Child Care

- Accounting

- Office Manager

- Administrator

- Assistant

- Clergy

- Police Officer

- Hotel Manager

- Salesman

- Event Organizer

- Hairstylist

- Makeup Artist

The ESFJs will feel happy doing any work that they like. And the jobs that make them feel happy are those that provide them opportunities to help others. They are not overly ambitious and career driven, they just want to have a harmonious working environment. Most of all, they will feel content in any job where they feel appreciated.

Chapter 5: The ESFJ's Workplace Behavior and Ethics

In the workplace, one can almost distinguish the ESFJs for their exceptional interpersonal skills. The ESFJs are warm, sociable, and nice! They make sure to talk to everyone in the workplace and that they know everyone by their first names. Remember that the ESFJs desire to be liked? They are indeed popular, and they use this trait to create a pleasant atmosphere in the workplace.

The ESFJ Subordinate

Individuals with this personality type are good followers. They don't just recognize rank and authority but give it their utmost respect. They follow rules in the workplace and they don't like to break laws. For their loyalty, ESFJ subordinates need to feel appreciated by their bosses. They thrive well in jobs where their hard work and dedication are recognized. However, the boss of an ESFJ may have a hard time with this subordinate when it comes to trying out new things at work. ESFJs are very traditional and they feel comfortable with orthodox ways. In case, of changes, they may have a hard time adjusting. Nevertheless, they can assimilate in time and once they understand how the new things work. Often, they will accept change just to keep the peace at work.

The ESFJ Colleague

A lot of value is placed on ESFJ colleagues. They help create a friendly atmosphere in the workplace and they make everyone feel comfortable. People with the ESFJ personality type are kind and generous, so they will help a colleague in any way they can. These folks are good workers, so they will always do their share of the load. When there are tasks that require teamwork, ESFJs have no trouble cooperating with their colleagues. Actually, they might enjoy the interaction more than the actual work. Putting the ESFJ in a job where he works alone can inhibit his energy and productivity. They are most productive when they are working in close quarters with other people.

The ESFJ Manager

A person with the ESFJ personality type experiences real pleasure in being in-charge, especially when it comes to organizing social gatherings. They have this opportunity when they are placed in positions of authority. By being the head of a team, the ESFJ can plan and organize, interact with numerous persons, and have the power to create peaceful, pleasant, and enjoyable environments. Whether they are planning a business meeting, a party, or a small dinner for the family, the ESFJ never fails to wow his audience. He has a knack for creating situations that make people comfortable and happy.

As managers, the ESFJ is never dominating or intimidating but quite the opposite; ESFJ manager can be friendly and accommodating. However, he is also traditional, so he will not appreciate subordinates that cross the line or disrespect the authority of the boss. For the ESFJ manager, there should always be a firm line between the boss and the subordinate. ESFJ leaders are effective because they inspire people to be optimistic and to work harder in order to attain their goals.

In the workplace, the ESFJs are always considered valuable members. They are pleasant to be around and they get the work done. They are never in a conflict with anyone and especially never with the company that they work for. Their work values are exceptional and they strive to uphold rules and traditions. Whether the ESFJ holds a managerial position or works as a subordinate, he will still be a productive member of the team.

Conclusion

The ESFJs will always be recognized for their friendliness and their caring attitude. When thrown in a room full of new people, the ESFJs will always be the ones to break the ice. They can make people feel comfortable just by saying a few friendly words. Mainly, it's their happy countenance that helps people to relax and to just put their guard down. Because of their sociability, the ESFJs are pretty popular wherever they go.

In their careers, the ESFJ are also a hit. They are able to make their mark in their chosen careers for their exceptional administrative and social skills. Because of these great traits, the ESFJ individual will never have a hard time making new friends and rising in the careers they've chosen. They have a good working attitude and they respect tradition and authority. These traits make them efficient and productive workers.

As lovers, the ESFJs make wonderful husbands or wives, boyfriends or girlfriends. They are innately caring and they are always attuned to the needs of their partners. For them, love and commitment are very important, so they will always put their time and effort into keeping their romantic relationships happy and secure.

The one thing that the ESFJ individual needs is appreciation from his friends, family, lover, and colleagues. Without reassurance from the people he cares about, the ESFJ may lose confidence in himself and could become a person that tries too hard to win other people's approval. In order to keep the ESFJ happy in any kind of relationship, whether its business, family, friendship, or romance, he will need to hear words of praise. This gives him affirmation that he is doing good and that he is someone that is considered important by those around him. ESFJs that fail to get the recognition and appreciation that they need may become very unhappy and eventually unproductive individuals. The ESFJs thrive on approval and appreciation from family, friends, colleagues, and from that special someone. When the ESFJ feels loved, he can be the best person there is.

You have been reading about the traits of the ESFJ— his strengths and weaknesses. By digesting this information, one can arrive at good conclusions for the best careers for the ESFJ as well as the most suitable personality types for a romantic partner. If you are an ESFJ, then I hope that I have given you a better understanding of your personality type. Hopefully, you can use what you've read in determining the right careers for you. And if you know someone who has this personality type, then consider yourself armed with valuable information. After all, it's an advantage to know what makes other people tick.

Finally, I'd like to thank you for purchasing this book! If you enjoyed it or found it helpful, I'd greatly appreciate it if you'd take a moment to leave a review on Amazon. Thank you!

Made in the USA
Middletown, DE
20 March 2021